Evil Summer

By Matt Snee

Copyright 2024 by Matt Snee

This tale of hospitalization and suicide, love and death, is meant for those who suffer the same, and it is hoped these words carry you through to the light, as they did me.

For Qin

<u>More Snow</u>

More snow.
I've been here for twenty-four days,
imprisoned, in a hospital,
for my own safety.

There are penguins, tigers, clamorous bells;
all disguised as humans: some as nurses,
and some as other patients.
They are busy monsters in paranoid hallways.

"I'm not here to take anything from you."

Shafts of rope quiver in the amiable city,
her rope, her city,
her voice over the phone asking if I am all right,
revealing the solemn caresses of staggering suns,
the bountiful trembling of her scrawny tears,
the infernal sculptor and the terrible dawn of her death.

Her brain was full of fire:
"Ocean, I hate you. Ideas: thin air!"

Still it snows, despite the summer,
and distant climaxes form a monotone tower,
a tireless, torrid heart that brays from beyond the moon.

One must beware
when confronting the congealing nothingness,
the chaste crumbling stars,
the stupor of horizons,
the empurpled hope of dusk.

Rebellious flesh, dreaming of her body,
even now,
her hair soft in my hands like black flowers.
I remember many things —
What now?
What else?
Should I go or remain?

We were fond of misery,
despisers of the Gods,
so intent to see nothing else.
Her beauty confesses the old despair
in the twilight shade of tangled thickets.

The paradox is obvious:

Endless contests.
Golden illusions flung in the way.

And all I can say to her,
in the last conversation we have
before she dies:
"Leave me asleep."

<u>Harvest</u>

Both gross and mystical,
the malformed city whispers
"conformity,"
with its granite tongue.

Philadelphia.

Here she lived, fighting off intimacy,
fucking strangers, neglecting friends and family.
Vain muscles, flames, murderous hounds:
What is the password?

Long ago I held her,
under the green silk moon,
surrounded by the city.
Like some great wave,
she had already drowned me

I was hers;
forever.

She was a timid hunter though,
her feet stepping across twigs of secrets
beneath the moon's gibberish.
I saw her —
there were stacks of voices and lashing faces,
omnivorous,
in the immense embryo of her despair.

Her army halted;
the enemy was unknown,
and words are full of danger in their foaming power,
their careful perfume.

There I found her in the ominous orchard
of the radiant, balmy Earth,
surrounded by the fears of old, a charnel of treachery,
forming the turbid history of us two sad apes.

I am saturated with lonely summons
in a soundless eternity.

She hated: Complacent music.
She hated: Crippled throats.
She asked: "What is the sky?"
The world answered: "Mother's roof."

Rise together against the old law.
The coffin?
A miracle.

<u>Skull</u>

Elated hours like hair being combed in a mirror.
Pity me not — the knife is warm.
She asphyxiates herself,
with a forlorn determination.

Her lovely voice: "Storms pass. So do I."

My skin can feel the pearly outlines
of an unscripted tragedy.
Cherry-colored shark.

That age is gone.
He stole her away to tattered hills and hanging shores,
bashful thoughts;
singing adventure among the whirling apparitions
of the heart's ecstasy.
She is lifted, free,
gone to the safe torture of great waves
and edgeless nudity.

Magic peach: Where is your toothed brain now?

Ashes linger.
This poem of neon Venus and green Earth
flames in the moment,
and then it all flows back to the sea,
intact, surrendering, lifted.

My vacation in reality includes drums, trumpets,
and an audience.
What an incredible waste.

<u>**Wheel of Fire, Wheel of Water**</u>

The Earth is a criminal,
ravishing, fumbling,
a goblet drinking.
We are insects
trapped inside its glass;
singing about what might have been,
bone and light,
a strange hunger sleeping in our kisses,
a poverty words cannot tell.

We need a warning.

There is a present to open:
it is called "the sky."
There is:
more mud to crawl through on our bellies.

Fruit of tongues cast upon the floors of basements,

long walks through the city, feet blistered, arms bound,
eyes bludgeoned by spiraling jets of discord.

Phantoms. Smoke.
Things that are almost human reach out —

She was a passenger – but to where?

The Tyrant of Miles Unknown

Profit and death:
yearning mercies,
sweet harbors.
She adored purpose.

Her lover, the Tyrant, and I never meet.
I only hear stories of him,
of his cruelty,
of his sexual amazements,
of his money.

Stone has grown around my lips.
My eyes have turned gray.
The dead are witnesses to hopelessness.
"They are waiting."

Little clockwork, I love you,
the cup of you, the dwindling paths of you,

your immoral language,
you are a silver island of babbling flesh,
a shooting star asleep.

Nothing in her life was accidental.
Her skin was an hourglass, an axis,
sour sunlight in a memorized tunnel, oblivion.
She explored it, recklessly,
shared it, withheld it,
clutched in time,
her darkest darkness
a painful freedom.

Picture the depths of my ragged father,
trying to catch the wind in his hands
among indecipherable innuendos
and a plague of memories.
Purple meadows, desolate, unfinished;
hounding caves; quaint nonsense; encounters;
baubles —

I fought the world beneath the sulking sapphire sky,
but she would never be mine.
He was the Tyrant of miles unknown,
an older man who greedily sucked at her youth,
clean, rich, with a son he didn't love
and a vengeful confidence.

I will not confess.

Swinger parties. Anal sex. Whip and clamps.
She inhaled all of it, thrilled.

I will not confess.

The Music

She is gone.

Is this what I am given,
to preserve this residue of silent shudders
and useless rituals of sorrow?
What good is in this body?

The day has begun
and I am no longer mourning
inside my temple of boundaries.
Doors close;
a lake of curious, stemmed metal
rises out of dirty pastures,
a wild spirit or an obscure wound — no, a gray mask.

God is not God,
chunks of a lion grappling cities,

an ill garden of mad rainbows,
a clutter of souls peering into the chasm.
Summer caught us in its jungle milk.

The spice of her was never so sweet.

Fear not the end, that vexing,
unpalatable ambiguity.
Fear not the small wrong
that melts the primitive heaven,
the mind revealed.
We make our own winter.

She speaks:
"I've gone on ahead."

A dripping error strewed over everything:
what remains of her immortal factory,
and the profound music
thrashing in her astonishing heart?

<u>Why Not Me?</u>

Impatient inorganics crowd the horizons around her.

"Who is willing to worship the stars and sun again?"
she asks.
"Who is willing to enjoy a melancholy
that time cannot bend?"

"Is there nothing older than Hell?"

Only hope.

There is a round, screeching sorrow that unfolds
beneath the sky along the nervous Earth.
Scared drums talk and squirm
in a trembling voice beneath my skin.
I'm broke, scarred.
What should I cling to?

To her?

Deliberate years form a triangle around us,
stealing away my courage,
and whatever anarchy lays within me.

(It's love! It's love!)

Another withered present, cajoling,
loose like a wild predator clawing at your back.

But her,
a crumbling, ancient song,
a war that never sleeps,
she stumbles towards me in her skirt,
long legs bare,
then up the stairs,
I'm behind her as she ascends,
her thighs at my eye level,
she turns back to look at me and smiles.

This futuristic landscape is not free from complaint.
The glimmer fails, like a mutating wish;
night has come truly now, galloping in,
half-wooed and half-spurned;
flood and drought at once.

She had seen the other planets in her sleep,
she had seen them trembling as they wait for us,

in agony,
their virgin soils both aged and ageless.
They wait for us to scale the sky as we scaled the sea,
behind a gnashing fog of shining black mud.
The sun moans;
we will spin leviathans of metal from this Earth
and climb further into the strange.

But her,
she bloomed at night,
and now she has entered the night,
forever.

"I'm a pioneer," she says in her suicide note,
"I'm going on ahead."
"I'll meet you there, you'll see."

These are my rational reasons
to explain my irrational feelings.
Things are falling down fast, so dream with me,
while we can.

My plan is to run.

Staircase

"It is better to be lonesome
than to mix with the fools of the Earth."
For such thoughts
there are sleeping pills
and racing cars.

Bred amongst monsters,
God is my favorite science,
sitting lonely in the river water,
the candle that never lights.

Did she believe?
I can't believe anything
but that she *did*.

I had a vision of her in the wild hours of the dark.
From some odd corner of my brain it flew,

carrying with it roaring gloom, blackness, and mire;
and here I, ripe for birth, became its smile.

The black Earth broods.
Meteors strike palaces of crystal.
"Where does the path lead?"

Men come and go.
Their feats mean nothing.
Their hearts like fistfuls of mud.
What matter if I go mad?

The echoing spirit is a blot.
I've never tasted love
and it's never tasted me,
like two dragons asleep in a dark cave.

I had a vision of a startling song,
lovelier than the tumult of morning.
I've never been silenced by the magic,
never been between the cliff and the wave.
Pure I am, still,
after long eternities
like wind in the Autumn,
like a long itching door.

The world weeps beneath a mantle of shadow.
I weep beneath a dirt of hope.
"The path leads nowhere."

I had a vision of a fairy beach, violet and dewy.
I walked it and listened to the breath of the sea.
I found no rest.

The wild hours are filled with nameless trouble.
The path will speak.
"The path forks!"

I had a vision of a flight of stairs.
I turned away from it, frightened, nauseous.

It was not what you think.

<u>Young Hero</u>

Close the door on this rotting morning.
The chanting rain is shivering proof,
an unclouded mirror.

Dreams pierce like jubilant cymbals.
The slothful strength
of a million gems of ragged wisdom —
a specter in a hall.
Forgive me now, young lamb;
the branches bore a creamy summer.

Once upon a time I was a happy man,
half-awake, a dull dagger.
My windless manhood was a hidden tomb,
a muttering web built on a humming verge.
Until the flickering bliss
of being at the threshold of the vault of her,
trampled my thoughts,

and I found myself a wreath of systems,
pulsing crimson in the unfaithful orbits
of this savage sphere.

We are all meek idols to the lips of a meadow,
twilight castles and friendly heavens
in the hands of a destructive mechanic,
where punished angels wrestle with fame
and horned time.
Too many fail in this braid of thorns and light,
and any memory of anguish is an intense sickness,
a haunting glimpse of old beasts
and their foreboding vapors.

Cruel, cruel world, modern Earth,
torrential day, immortal mimic;
its immortal mimic plays at a mortal harp,
plucking a cheap melodic freedom,
an aloof wounding of robed flame.

There is no end to her steaming secrets,
no end to the thrones of moss and raving purples,
no end to the wandering silences
and undrainable stars.

The sullen city KNOWS.
The slumbering child is but a fragment,
a murmur of the drum.

"But to look upon a whisper!"

I don't believe it.
We chained ourselves into this menial age,
and there is no more flight in me.

But don't forget this:
where there is a door there is a place to venture into.

Young lamb,
you would be a fool to crawl into
and sleep in the tyrant's hand.
I depart, young lamb.
I burn.

Great sorrow. Great sorrow.

Lonely Conqueror

She was an unimaginable veteran,
rising slowly in an evening crowd of second thoughts.
She wandered; it was all home to her.
She threw herself into the hot theater
of the Right Now.
I took shelter in her, in her shadows, in her skin,
in the elegant viper of her smile.

Paralyzing; the verdant flame,
the ceiling.
So placid a voice to ring from the heavens,
so harmonious.
I return to myself.

Beyond me there is a sum of lines,
some sober, some madly naked.
Midnight chugs like an engine around me,
and no matter how many steps I take I get nowhere.

I sit to rest.
I have grown less complex, somehow.
I have become a scaled lizard with a heart of fire.
I snort smoke and my wings ache.
Under the plumed sky I pluck deer from forests.
In the tender atmosphere I breathe
like any other machine.

"She is dead, then?"
She is dead.
All the round Earth knows.
The sky spits me out, my wings shrivel,
and I'm stuck on the ground.
What tyranny!

"I am dead, then?"
I am dead.
Do not lecture me on the quenching language of love.
Do not lecture me on the vain sports of men.
Now the cold breeze lurks beneath my skin;
I have become brittle.

Take me back.
Take me back to how it was with her,
when the wing carried me into the clouds
beneath the secret sun.
Close my eyes to this field of tears
and melancholy wind;
I have never seen anything I have hated so.

Lonely conqueror,
riding out of the ruins of night:
let me go.

<u>**Footsteps**</u>

Flames chew the sky.
No creed could stop her;
no germ of meaning could make this a gentle home.

Stern Gods gather on the voluptuous shore,
spawning smiles and mellow amazement.
The long shock of shameful thunder
makes for the foundation of a barren sleep,
malignant foliage in the shiny yonder.

It's the most blessed trick;
that her diamond face can shine through this thin darkness
and reach my mystic eye
through the crumpled sheathing of my ghostly bottle.

A calm helplessness is disastrous medicine,
spurning confusion in our burnt culture
and its veiled wars.

I heard her silken groaning,
I heard the beating planet,
I heard the misty flutes of the vanished desert;
a pleasant relic in this strange gulf of stolen moods.
Have patience:
the silver features of a boundless noon
form the shell of a lullaby,
an ungrateful altar worth forgetting.

These are footsteps of a cycle
that has no order and no serene conclusion;
only perplexing vastness and a vacant hunger
in the shape of death.
We are molten isles, mirages of electric hope
tending calamity, brute woe, and delicate horror.

The bellowing cells of my body are born dangerous,
a waking worm embracing the yellow curtain
of this satin Eden and all that the year requires.

The fairest grain can shatter the long hoof of time,
and we can find ourselves overthrown
by the promised flaw.

Prideful maggot: your splendid lust is a stubborn villain
clothed in wolfish flame,
a little onslaught at the base of a jealous mountain.
A storm is coming.

Must I die?
I am only a simple container for imperial waste,
writhing in the silent chapel
of her sleek mouth.
She was my marvelous prize.
Thank you for her violation of my underground realm.
Thank you for her weeping horn.

Still, this fragile shell has a noble force
that is its burden in the sundered void.
She was a foolish warrior among lawless creatures,
unwelcome wealth that was a spry leaf
sailing across a dismal glass.

The moon is a smiling knife in a roan sky,
a fancy lie that allows me to catch my breath,
a polluted farewell in the traitorous deep.

A repeating defect.

The Astounded Prisoner

"The sun shines on the just and unjust alike,"
says the astounded prisoner
to the cave of voices.
The cold chemicals
of newborn emotion
are comically smeared about her.
From here there is no return,
and the obedient crowd of moonlit despair
makes her an icy daughter.

The neglected sunset pushes over tired sand
through a shining field of wind and impatient splendor.
She is a merry mercenary in the red stillness.
"Keep calm." — a brave notion.
Parched swallowing compels strange motives,
devouring her crippled panic in a grinding womb.

They were all lies,
a sleepy licking of cozy memories,

a wreck of miracles locked in a dancing margin
of the miserable upstairs,
private trophies for our gang of egos.

The legendary foe has an urgent name.
The devil is in the details,
in the plump salt of flesh,
and the eternal magic of crawling dread;
an occasional doom
roaming the squalid pewter of the soul.

Precious terror,
were that you of sturdier elements.
The harsh games of prosperous swords never cease
in the tangled spasms of the ivory awake.
She was murdered in a circular instant;
and rots in the sinister caress of its whirling zenith.

Mere centuries are no potion for this staring dragon.
A wasp of color is a somber nurse
in the sunless lands of the dead,
poison beckoning a mangled dynasty
of desiccated horizons;
curious nourishment for roses
shedding feigned rope.

<u>Her</u>

The water is still poisoned,
the sky is still in doubt,
and I still don't know where you are.
There is no retreat from your absence.
Its anxious beak will not be denied.

The calm before this is legendary,
a summer flame lingering through the night,
a rapid river that sang through the spheres,
the ripest echo I have ever known.

The salt of blood will purify anything.
Morning songs ring across lost plains of amber,
high cliffs that rise over the sea.
What did Eve say to her daughters?

In those days I wore a suit and tie

and rode trains through tunnels.
With all our miracles, still only this,
this habitual longing
transferred into gray plastics and throbbing coppers,
a serrated glittering, clutched
in sweaty palms and stabbing hearts.

I will entertain your ancient harp like a raft
upon the ocean,
I will tear you like a voice,
I will be a shower of rain across your brow.
No one compares to you.
"I love you."
I love you, all of you,
every death of you,
every somebody that you are
in the haze of this net.
I will give you no menace,
I will drown in your unspeakable sum.

"I love you."
I love you,
your hungry wind,
the monarch of your embrace.
Enter my city and be my meteorite.

<u>**Evil River**</u>

She peels away the skin
that keeps her from seeing God.
She peels away the scrawled road
of a torch extinguished.
She abandons the slope and the vulgar toil.

"Who were you before you died?"

A poem forgotten.
She was breathing, lingering spirits.
She travelled in vain.
She enjoyed the flaming comfort
of TRUE EXPERIENCE.

"I cannot find the way alone."

Night had set foot in her brain,
and the feeble labyrinth of this mortal fever
became a strange teardrop and a sad lesson.
Between truth and reason lies a black atmosphere,
a great wretchedness.

Enjoy the hideous solace of your sophist's zeal.
Terrible as lightning,
these gushing ashes make a primal veil
for the regions of sorrow.
Child of memory, filthy hog,
roaring organ:
your corrupt testimony bursts apart
under my bitter footsteps.

There is one vast realm of reckless moments,
a divine coil, a strange eternity.
Here we dwell in the lava of hectic days
and imagine we can control the void.

There is a majestic distortion in the flush of the dawn.
There is a pleasant abyss,
where crumbled friends await,
where the sun goes to its nest with a groan
and the plague of time disappears in a vengeful flash.
There is a crevice with a noble shape
that says nothing of the winged error,
and the horrible currents cease.

A simple life, in a doorway,
beneath a huge sky,
bereft of shaggy whispering and somber pipes,
free of plainness and rash misery.

A delightful chaos.
A trembling pinnacle.
An evil river.

<u>The Colossal Deformity</u>

The colossal deformity hates itself –
obviously.
It hates everything, hates me and hates you.
This hate is a fiery liquid
in the veins of its centipedal limbs
and drooling mouths —
an impervious cloud.
From father to son it rots, transparently.

There is an eloquent pyramid of foreign guardians
who speak with imperial lips.
They hold us down from behind
and make us choke on their medicine.
"These are the conditions of truth," they say.

Just as it was before.
There is a vomiting heat, a deep wound.

There is a sleepless dog in my iron throat.
There are inspiring despots in this sedate kingdom,
where your frail rage
is a starry nectar for inhuman skeletons
made of tungsten and copper.

We were silent
and treated this ghost as a solid thing.
We were enclosed; dead.
We were killed in a wild surprise.

Memory misleads in the reign of the cave.
The deceptive weight of reason
has abandoned the blind fabric of the real world,
and the fervor of the ancient wandering
revives like an evil servant of bottomless design,
a butcher with a divine burden,
a pagan harmony of beautiful hunger and leafy voices.

Here,
the eager teeth of twisted mountains mangle the sky
in thirsty welcome,
a red gluttony in innocent air.
The bending branch envelops the boiling heart
in its tart forest of living sound,
the slave ocean and the free ocean meet in muzzled lust,
and sing in a distant harness
of entropic rhyme.

I am a proud heretic
ready to ascend to the stars.

The Baffled Wraith

There is a smiling tide of ruined silence:
the prize of her suffering.
She is a slumbering violin
in a clenched universe.

She sought a guiltless fame,
a soothing paste of vain dungeons,
a sneering havoc.
This was her shard of the question.
This was her sacred fretwork of the baffled wraith.
Like a thawing atom
she receded into sleeping shadow,
a portion of the summit reflected in our accursed gaze.
No peril frightened her.

It is an awful season
for such loyal desolation.

The naked throb of this pompous disaster is suffocating,
a sweet speck of a dark wealth,
a cauldron of sickly beauty.

"Paradise awaits forgotten heroes."

So the tangled strength of boundless hours.
There is no escape from this atrocious child,
the awful grasp of a malady of envy wrapped tight
in the private juices of her scarlet ore,
a remnant of shrill twilight and uncorrupted emotion
in her reluctant body.
So is the injured winter in her grove of walls,
her haggard past dissolved
in the remedy of summoned wilderness.

Nothing but cold snow.

There is a spectator captive
to the odd portal of her impervious thought.
There is a chamber of adamant spirals
sheltered beneath her savage wing.
There is a splinter of the throttle
calmly mentioning her name across the sky.
There is a sublime sore,
scribbling pale tremors of sensation
across the alloy of her burden of arrogance.

Providence, like a star, dripping gloom across her brow.

She had become a demon in act but a god in face.
She had become a soaring mold.

And her voice: "I did not seek to be born."

My mind overwhelms me.

A Drowsy Glimpse Into a Fantastic Suicide

To begin at the beginning
is like a drowsy glimpse
into a fantastic suicide.
I don't care who you are;
matter cannot comprehend spirit.

A moment's charms with her are an acute dirt.
There are thousands of moons,
millions of moons, billions of moons;
are they all galloping answers,
sighing pathways deathlessly bellowing fortune's tones?
Yes.
It is the divine embarrassment of the control-less core.

There is a sparkling worm in the sky.
There are gigantic shadows

that shut us out of the ethereal purple.
There is a reptile's subtlety
that still forms a severe cloud
around we who share the apple.
There is a pale army of wheels in the primal stream.
There is a ferocious suspicion in the greedy pit
of the mortal way.

Palisades of a fever.
A delirious concert of material anxiety.
A terrifying buzz of permanent yellow.
The axis of a benign operator's transparent nature.
The spell of a suffering dynamic.

I can't get over the helpless fact of it,
the stitched drool of a sacred spectrum
of wet silence and expensive bones.
Things hang together somehow between moments,
locked up in a honeycomb structure.
There will be an abandoned parade of hissing technology,
the simian galaxy stranded
in the scummed doubt of anxious daylight
and the mountain of night.
To understand darkness and its temperatures –
weeping fingers of a sour freedom,
a torpor of pretty apparatus
crisply speaking through the long hour.

Was I mistaken?

Was my windward intellect drowned
in the straggling tribe of the invisible?
Have I wandered home at last?
Have I come to begin?

<u>Everything Is In Sight</u>

There is a little more left.
There is a quivering sky in my head,
an assembly line of human caves and chopping rooms.
There is a devouring oxygen like a criminal
in the flute of time.
Speech swarms about us.
Everything is in sight.

My ruined tongue is empty now.
Wet metal grows idle and inhales the stars.
I hear a whispering.
This particular omen is unlike the others.

I am a passenger.

I am looking for something.
I am a frozen wind stretched beyond its limits.
I am the path undecided.

There is a true, palpable dark.
I have held its spinning core.
I have romanced through a lifetime of cold light
and unattainable forevers,
and though I am no stranger to music,
I have belonged to the long bitterness
of conflagrated lines.

There is a crystal clear bell,
that I can hear,
sounding from somewhere on the other side of the ocean.
I will not follow.
I will not.

Maybe there will be a time for you and me, my love;
and I will pet the wood of your skin
and kiss your holes long into the meadow.
Your voice will drown out all else,
and I will float among you.
This is a dream, this is no dream.
This is an eyelid, fluttering in the rays of the sun,
entombed in the rampant sky.
We will be fabled things, my love;
and I will make your every day a soft river
that's easy to memorize and repeat.

<u>Final Sky</u>

Say "the wound is healed," and it is healed.
A statue born in the bulb of darkness,
looking for your mothy reward,
quivering in the entrance of your lonely realm;
in the creator's torchlight you find pieces of a surface,
and forgotten evenings.

The light is frail,
a brocade of sharp clouds
rings the profound jewel of the sun.
"I am heir to the jungle."

Born in empire,
in a grinning gutter or zealous facades,
the lost Autumns of a fallen century,
devoid of sleep, devoid of a barking eye;
a whorl of blinding delirium,
a sphinx of crackling bursts of windless thought.

Death will come.
Death will come like a menacing season
through the skyward mechanics of living gravity;
the helixed firmament of the rasping paradise,
where centaurs step through the moist ripples
of the forgotten source.

Death will come on a meaningless day,
to the door at the edge of a trance,
a sleeping precipice of whispering needles.

Saturn, the old God,
golden city of vomit, invading ink in the clicking vacuum,
orphaned epilogue, eternity's enemy, unleashed principle –
only a bloated echo of a peeling thorn,
an unfurled god on a bellowing plain,
a useless shape in the heap of blue.

I thought I had died in the octopus of thought,
accelerating,
the loom a foggy snake of abandoned sorrows.
Nothing mattered in that stubborn gray,
the cruel judge like a piece of rain,
a horrible telescope;
and the naked marvel of the shredded flood
was a machine-gun,
a foul ballet of white motion,
an alien mirror.

Love's blade is a soaring reservoir of blazing palaces,
naked ruins of feet and wings,
the demented populace's jagged victory.
I endure.
Dissolving insects assume transformation
in the evil belly of enormous progress,
barricaded behind the entombed reflections
of unfinished astronomy,
a betrayal coveted by a poised sickle.

This, resembling a metamorphosis,
resembling a breathless time
with a rattling texture of incorporeal diameters,
a morose cone of limitless marble,
an unattended winter in the animal stratosphere,
where the humble gold of caustic sunsets
form dream's mouth and say:

"It's just the conquering ocean. It's just the republic."

Toys and treasure,
a reckless bosom's decrepit future;
the reeking flare of an electric afterlife;
a vast movie of defiant rope,
an immaculate distance.

But say "the wound is healed," and it is healed.

The pious metal of a penned fate is a corrupt substance,
bewitching ribbons of a world of spirits.
All walls are vulgar;
far and near the eternal obstacle's glow lingers,
and the beautiful cripple of your tolling anatomy
is a dangling melody in the broke weather
of smashed fancy.

This purple-curtained prison
is an ogre of tiptoeing light,
a torrent of patterns of immortal information;
a barefoot, wondrous fluid
older than Rome.

The translucent Earth is the brightest road
in the dusty grief of the Great Danger.
We wander ashore,
into the fold of the elastic marsh,
a pile of thirsts in the dark abdomen of this mad corridor.
The deluded flea is an anguished creature,
noon teeth forsaken by the slippery grape
of stammering freedom.

The vague ice is a fairy monument,
the pale coral of a parasitic molecule,
a cannibal, a fathomlessly dark machine.
The story goes on. In this secret winter
there is the scavenged ignition of an extravagant flame,
a ticking ravine, a sugary piano of dying tears,

a devious amulet of immoral blueprints.
There is a vicious blackness,
a mystery of the coughing architect
that the lizard knew;
but the melancholic ape – curious always –
is nervous bait in its devouring farewell.

Dim, grim origin: the remote geology of the wound.
But say "the wound is healed" and –
It is healed.

Matt Snee was born in Nebraska and raised in Delaware. He is a self-taught writer, painter, musician, and cartoonist. He currently lives in Phoenix, Arizona.

www.ingramcontent.com/pod-product-compliance
Lightning Source LLC
Chambersburg PA
CBHW030403160726
47992CB00007B/2940